Graced In His Presence

Published by:

WRITE-ON CHAPBOOKS
A DIVISION OF WRITE-ON PUBLISHING

59 Tom Brown Boulevard,
St Francis Bay 6312
Tel: +27(0)422941023
frank@writeonpublishing.co.za
www.writeonchapbooks.co.za

Edited by Frank Nunan
Cover & Book Design: Frank Nunan

Contact: Hlengiwe Mngadi: mngadi.hlengiwe@gmail.com

ISBN: 978-1-990944-85-7

Graced In His Presence

By Hlengiwe Mngadi

About the Poet

I am Hlengiwe Mngadi and I was born on 31 October 1985.

I live at Enkanyisweni Area (Umbumbulu ward) on the South West of Durban.

I studied Psychology (specialising in counselling) at UNISA Durban, and I have a BA in Human Sciences and Social Services, specialising in Psychological counselling.

I further studied towards and  obtained my PGCE (Postgraduate Certificate in Education), specialising in teaching Languages and Life Orientation, from UNISA.

After that I obtained an Honours Degree in Educational Management (UNISA) and have not stopped pursuing my studies.

I also hold an IC3 Spark Certificate in computing from the Durban University of Technology.

I am employed as an educator, teaching Languages and Life Orientation at Emtshibeni High School, and I constantly engage with my students with counselling sessions as the need arises.

I grew up being a very quiet and reserved child even though I had siblings; therefore, I learned to express myself and my thoughts in writing. However, my calling or my gift as a counsellor and a teacher has been evident before I even began to study. Above all else, I love spending my time reading the Word of God, meditating on it and writing.

Table of Contents

Dedication & Acknowledgments

To my Heavenly Father, the giver of life, gifts, talents, wisdom, understanding and courage to exercise our gifts for His glory.

To my spiritual father, LV Mahlangu (the Founder of Kingdom Embassy International Church and an outreach Ministry called LV Ministries) who has been teaching me and others the Word of God tirelessly. My mentor, my life coach. Through him, I have learned the power of meditation and the importance of fellowship with God, as well as with fellow humans. He has taught me the importance of exercising spiritual gifts and talents. He has been working tirelessly, being used by God for my deliverance, Salvation and all God's blessings. *Matthew 11:28*. Indeed I was weary and heavily burdened, but now I am free indeed.

To the Cele family, they have always believed in me even when I didn't believe in myself that much, and they always encourage me to press on, even in the midst of challenges.

To my best friend, Stanley. He has never stopped encouraging me to write and each time I feel discouraged, he always has a word to boost my faith. His words make me walk tall and to realise that nothing is out of reach, as long as you can imagine it, you can be it, for with God, all things are possible. "Many waters cannot quench love, nor can rivers drown it." *Songs of Songs 8:7*. Hence my love to write was restored, and courage to finally get my book published. I promise you, my friend, that this is one of many more books that will be published, for nothing may quench my love to do the will of God.

To my brother, Sphelele, you have been my brother and my friend.

To my Mom and Dad, who allowed God to use them as a vehicle, to deliver me to planet earth. My family, brothers and sisters who have never stopped wishing me well and supporting me.

To all those who have not yet started pursuing the purpose of God for their lives, I encourage you to find the purpose and run with it before you can grow old and complain of lack of fulfillment. The purpose can be realised through fellowship with God. Your gift will make a way for you to be seated with kings in high places.

8

My Fatherless Generation

If my Father were absent,
Surely I would be food for jackals,
a subject to scorn
if it were my foes, attacking me
I understand
but my brother who shares my bread,
I don't understand
If my Father is absent, who will wipe all
  these tears,
and have my wound dressed up?
So deep my wound, yet they treat it lightly
Saying, all is well
 In the absence of my Father,
A causeless curse might follow and overtake
  me
And since mine father knows me by name,
Curses are broken
No one cared for you at birth; your
  umbilical cord remained uncut
Bound in all aspects of this lifetime,
You disregarded your Father's commands
Turn and go back to your Father in
  repentance,
You shall live
For what Father rejoices in the son's death?
Go back to your former life and rise to fall
  no more.

On His 26th Birthday

This is a song about my Father
Listen to him and search not for another
These are the words from my Father
"Come and drink from the words of
  wisdom."
Come to me all you who are weary and find
  rest
Listen to the song from my father and just
  dance to the tune
He found me when I was broken
Heavens above know I was rotten
Somehow I felt I was forgotten
Suddenly dawn creeps from mountain
  heights to valleys of dry bones
A loud voice came as though from heavens
  above
"Arise dear princess arise
For your light has come
Why must you lie dead in your sins?
For your Daddy rejoices not in your death."
A sound of victory was heard,
"Here I come Master!"
Where will I go and worship thee?
My heart leaps for joy,
as I hear the sound of chains breaking
Indeed my Light has come
It is a new dawn.

A Woman Who Has Moved Beyond Her Past

She smiles in the face of afflictions
Kneels as though defeated but to draw
   strength from her father.
She hides not her wounds to spare you.
She doesn't mind letting you touch.
If only you would believe.
This woman has moved beyond her past.

Not known for many words, but her
   influence in her silences,
She is wise beyond measure but as humble
   as a lamb before its shearers.
Though a leader, she excels in foundations
and lets you step on her to shine.
She is no limelight kind of a woman, but the
   light walks before and after her .
She boasts not in her triumphs, but all in
   her weaknesses
 This woman has moved beyond her past.

She forgives even when it hurts.
Letting go of the grievous wounds of the
   past to start anew.
This woman is amazing.
Blessed is a man who will discover a wife in
   her.
Even more blessed are the fruits of her womb.
This woman has moved beyond her past.

I can tell from her ability to rise above
    adversities,
And smiles even when it hurts.
This woman when she holds you, warmth
    and comfort speaks louder than words
She speaks louder in her deep silences of
    meditation.
She lies awake in the midst of the night
    interceding for you and me.
This woman has moved beyond her past.

As weak as she may seem to be, but she is a
    prayer warrior.
This woman has struck the Goliath of your
    generation through her wisdom.
Many are the weapons in her storeroom.
I've seen her using a tent peg to screw Sisera
    to death.
She is a tool in the hands of the Creator.
This woman has moved beyond her past.

She holds a clear speaking conscience,
not contaminated by useless speeches,
    gossips,
grudges and silly arguments
Her mind has been transformed,
 and covered by the blood of the Lamb.
She is submissive beyond measure,
and humility is her uniform.
This woman has moved beyond her past.

She contests not for attention,
for she has secured her place at her Master's
 feet.
This woman has risen above condemnation,
Not shaken by the troubles of this present
 age.
She runs to her refuge when troubles come.
She has moved beyond her past.
She loves unconditionally and selflessly for
 Christ is moulded in her.
She walks tall though trouble tries to pull
 her down ,
when men don't understand her, they
 criticise her, yet she understands.
She is a woman of prestige - a woman of
 Honour,
when she walks, she makes a statement.
For this woman has moved beyond her past.

Beautiful Words Stir My Heart

Beautiful words stir my heart
As I recite a poem about my lover
Streams of water gush down my throat
as I imagine His Kingdom
I close my eyes and See the Light shine
As dawn rushes down the mountainside
down the valleys low

Beautiful words stir my heart
As I think of my Master,
Where will I go to find Thee?
Along the years of my youth,
my heart sings a love song, as I think of
  Thee
my heart skips a beat, on midnight hour,
Windows of my soul lie open,
As I wait in patience for my lover,
As a bride adorned for her bridegroom,
So am I? Patiently waiting for thee
Lover of My Soul
A husband of my youth
A scent of your presence, worth more than
  an alabaster
Dare not turn your back on me or I will
  perish

Words of your utterance light up my paths
and guide my feet to righteousness
Where will I go to find Thee?
At the deep of the night. I lie awake
  thinking about Thee
I refuse to touch my food
As my heart longs for Thee
Where will I go to find Thee?
I was glad when they said," let us go to the
  house of my Master."

Beautiful words stir my heart as I meet
  Thee.

It Is Better To Get Married Than Burn With Passion

Naked I came, naked I am,
Before you I come
As we lay in the Garden of Eden
Neither Men nor Angel hath seen me in You
Skilfully embroidered within you,
Another bone of your bones
I gave birth to you though extracted from
   you
Wonderfully and fearfully I and He are
   made,
 in the image of God
Naked I was presented before you
In full light, you took the decision of being
   the bone of your bones
and flesh of your flesh
 If this love was blind, you would have been
   in ether,
when I was named by you,
Displayed before you,
but to love or to leave was your choice to
   make

A Men's perfection lies not in the absence of
   sin,
but in utter repentance and being declared
   not guilty by the Lord
Just like the clay in the hands of the Potter
   had fallen,
I slipped and had fallen to pay attention to
   the second voice.
All along the fruit was laid bare before my
   sight,
and yet after this, was found remarkable
   and pleasing to the eye,
just as I was presented before you as a
   precious flower in the centre of the garden,
So I brought the fruit to your attention and
   the choice was yours to indulge
Naked I came yet in need for a cover now
Found refuge in the leaves of trees, and yet
   you found us
Marriage is for all, yet not all shall marry
   or be given to marriage
They that chose to remain in celibacy for
   the sake of the Gospel,
Let them tell the good news
And yet, if I were you, I would rather
   marry, than burn with passion.

Caught Up

Behold the sound of a trumpet blown, can
be heard in higher Places
Come to me all you who are weary and
heavily burdened
But let not your hearts be hardened,
hear the sound of the one calling in the
desert
Do not let your hearts be troubled
when you see these signs rejoice,
in my Father's house, there are many
mansions
he's coming for you in the blink of an eye
You will be caught up to meet Him,
All who slept in faith will see Him
when you see the clouds forming, as though
heavy rain might pour
prepare the way of the one coming with the
clouds
the same way He ascended, then He shall
descend
only this time His feet won't touch the
ground,
if He comes tonight, will you be found in
faith?
repent and turn from your evil deeds
He is coming for, you to be with him,
and be like him

Enoch walked with God all the days of his
  life
in reverence for the Lord, he remained
  faithful
when troubles came he would sing.

I know I have a permanent building,
where human hands are not employed to
  build
walk in faith, stay in faith, be caught up in
  faith.
Just as Elijah paid attention to every move
  Elisha made
Follow Him closer, paying attention to His
  decrees
what then would you like to inherit from
  your Master?
For Elisha asked for imperishable treasures
There are crowns in store for those who
  endure many hardships
And stay in faith.
Return to your former love and be caught
  up to meet Him.

Let Me Kiss You Good-Bye

I have known you for a decade and a half.
Whenever I go there shall you be found
  next to me.
Thousands of miles travelled with hands
  held as one
Wherever you set your foot, mine shall
  follow,
Neither a single height found out of reach
  nor valley
Too low to get to
When I miss the mark, there shall you be
  found, caught up in my web of guilt
Wherever the sound of our heartbeats there
  shall we be
suddenly a voice calling me out was heard
And as I turned to see you in your deepest
  Slumber
Totally out of reach
Two go well in agreement, but this call is
  mine to answer
for two may be found in one bed, and yet
  only one taken away
just as Elijah and Elisha were divided by the
  chariot of fire
So are we?
Caught up in a cloud to be seen no more by
  nude eyes
a voice of the one calling in highest places
  could be heard

"Come out!"
Then I say, "Here I come, my Master."
I turned to see you with me, but none go
   together least they agree
This call is mine to answer
None puts a hand on a plough and turn
   back may be found fit for the service of the
   Kingdom.

Just as Abraham was called to depart from
   his household,
So was I?
Why must we fight, my lover?
Why must you be where I am?
This one journey is mine to travel.
Just as Naomi released Ruth to her destiny,
   for she had nothing left to give her
release me!
Better to part in peace, than to quarrel in
   disagreements
Why must we let these years go
   unaccounted for,
when we can
 count our blessings and move on
better to part in peace, than put you in a
   corner too small for you to travel
two paths lie before us; I commend you take
   another
For mine has been chosen...
So come, let us Kiss and Say Goodbye.

Marriages of Nudity

When two lie down together they keep
  warm
Who then may defeat and rip us apart?
A cord of three strands is not quickly
  broken
Rooted foundations are rarely shaken
My love for you is not mistaken
Mine Prince has fallen asleep,
deeper than skin deep I was founded in you
how glued I am to you, nobody knows
like a corded tattoo, engraved in you
If your eyes remain closed when you found
  the bone extracted from your bones,
this love would be blind
out of many you chose me and I say,
"Take this pledge of my love for you."
Let's get married in the nude.
All I am, all I was remains bare to you
not a single strand of my hair may miss
  your count
Even the fruit I ate, I didn't hide, I gave you
Willingly, you ate for I was found impossible
  to resist
The wounds I bear, I hide not to spare you.
If only you may touch and believe that I am
regardless of my disgrace, I'm highly
  regarded through His grace.

Divorce decree could have been issued, but
  how can this covenant be broken?
You know all about me and I'm just like you
as we abide in marriages of nudity
together or run for our lives when our
  running could find us
how then can I escape the bone of my bones,
  flesh of my flesh?
How long will you be gone, my love?
  Paradise is cold without you
Even the fruits of my womb restless within
  me,
What shall I do except to wait patiently in
  faith, for when you come
Let's get married in the nude.

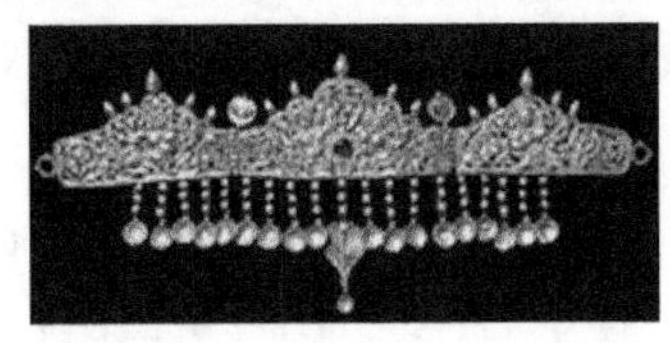

Save the Best for the Last Round

Now in my boat come stay with me,
Sit with me for a while longer
With dark dusk dive down the mountain
   heights.
Hiding from the face of this world, but I still
   see you with me
How I long for your tender arms around me
Like a shooting star, I'm caught up in the
   spark of your eyes
Illuminating my heart, filling me with
   overwhelming Splendour
How I wish this fire was readily kindled,
   keeping me warm all the days of my life.
Now in my boat come dine with me, with
   honeycomb sweeter than sweets.
Now the largest fish we caught calls for
   celebration and dancing
Come, let us drink and drown our sorrows
deep down the streams of waters.
Let us indulge in wine that satisfies and
   share the bread that liveth
Come let us delight in drinking and dance
   the night away in celebration of our
   freedom.
So in my boat calm the storm for me.
With our hands held kiss away the pain .

If only I could touch the hem of His garment
  then I know I'll be alright
If I could wash and wipe dry your feet with
  a kiss, then find my spot by your feet
Then I know I will find my joy.
Can I not as well save the best smiles for the
  morning time
Sorrow may last for the night and joy surely
  comes in the morning time

Like a swift breeze sweeping away my tears
  and fears
Shed the best tears for the last joy
Joyful moments of promotion
Save the last dance for my Father
Swiftly gliding away from commotion.
If only I could dance for my Father surely I
  could do better than David,
For the present days, glory is brighter than
  the former glory.
If only I could touch the strings, this melody
  would echo in your heart
As we save the last step for our last dance.

The Journey of KEI

I've been married to Tera for longer than I
can recall
Such a sweet name I thought
Little did I know you are deadly
You brought me nothing but limitations,
  frustrations,
Failure, backwardness, you name it
My entire generation suffered the scorn of
  my cruel husband
In 2013 Tera died a tragic death!
may his soul burn in hell
didn't bother attending the funeral
for I was too busy preparing to see the glory
  of God.
After the year Tera died,
I saw the glory of God as it was revealed in
  the year 2014
<u>as was proclaimed by my father LV
  Mahlangu</u>
I saw fire fall from Heaven when all
  mountains collapsed
and valleys lifted up
In 2015 favour of the Lord fell upon me
Promoting me to bear lasting fruits of
  righteousness
How can I forget 2016 as he moved me to
  my next level?

Just as the bride prepared to kiss the
  bridegroom
He adorned me and ushered me to 2017
destroying every stubborn stronghold of
  witchcraft ahead
through him foundational generational
  curses are broken
hear the sound of a trumpet blow
proclaiming the shaking of foundations
And the truth remains, "foundations are
  corrected by the Lord".
Just when witches and wizards lose hold
  over my life
there was light in the year 2018
light has been with me and in me
as I'm continuously being fruitful towards
  the journey
of multiplication in five-folds, seven times
  seven times
and even a hundred fold
Good morning 2019!
Indeed it's a new dawn and I'm being
  fruitful
the Egyptians you saw beyond the Red Sea
  are to be seen no more.

For all had perished in pursuit of the
    firstborns of God
the Red Sea has become a ladder for me to
    climb on to my destination
Responding to His call to follow Him closer
I say, "Here I Am Lord, I will follow you
    closer from 2020
and for the rest of my years on Earth."

The Song I Sing in the Mountain Heights, I Sing in Valleys Low

I sing praises in joyful moments of
promotion, shout for joy
and enter His courts with songs of gratitude
for His love knows no magnitude
and His mercies endure for all times
I sing the songs of gladness in mountain
   heights,
When eggs and bacon laid wait for me
It was joy in the morning
When money filled my pocket, I count it
   fame
The best of livestock never seen before, I
   owned
Servants I sent around the globe, I call it
   favour
When friends and family gather in my
   house to celebrate, I sing
This is the song I sing in mountain heights
Suddenly a meeting was held in Heavenly
   places, in my absence
My Father does nothing without
   proclaiming
Yet this one thing was not brought to my
   attention

A court case was held, and I was handed
  over to my accuser,
Thus without trial, I was convicted
What then shall I do?
I sing in this valley of darkness, the former
  song of joy
I eat ashes for food and sit alone in darkness
the place of my livestock, has become my
  home
My dearest friends have been dogs licking
  my wounds
Even my dearest friends have turned
  against me
They accuse me of sins, I know not
Yet I sing a love song, in the depths of the
  valley
My lovely sons and daughters are gone to be
  seen no more
What then shall I say, the Lord had given
  the Lord had taken
Blessed be the name of the Lord.
My helper has turned against me.
Where then shall my help come from?
My help comes from the maker of all
  Universe
Shall then I curse my maker? Surely not I,
  Lord!
Shall I not acknowledge afflictions, as much
  as I've had my blessings to count?
The song I sing in mountain heights, I still
  sing it even louder now

Having been a laughing stock and public
  disgrace
My days have I cursed, yet the Lord I bless
"Where then is your God?" They ask me.
If in present day's life, I were to boast, my
  weakness I will show
Three times I pleaded with my Father, to
  remove my thorn in vain
What then shall I say? All is vanity under
  the sun
In vain I sing,
All the riches like smoke of breath soon
  vanishes
Just like a rose in the garden, I wither
The day of departure is better than the day
  of birth
and sorrow, than happiness,
for the broken-heartedness attracts God
Shall I then go on boasting of my reaches?
Both the poor and the rich sleep in death
  bed
how then shall I spend my days here on
  earth?
My robe, I shall soak in the blood of the
  Lamb
Then I shall see my maker when I breathe
  my last
and be like Him
Just as pure gold, I am refined in the place
  of the living
Then I sing the same song.

Under God's Eye

Behold the eye of the Lord cries over the city
Woe to the Shepherds that feed my flock
  tares instead of grass
I've set greener pastures for my flock,
and yet the blind leaders lead my sheep to
  the graveyard
They squander their wealth
and promise peace where there is no peace .
woe to the prophets who prophesy lies and
  put a seal on their statement
"Thus says the Lord,
if they have spent a day in my counsel,
I would have spoken to them, yet they
  spread lies on my name
They dress the wound of my people as
  though shallow,
saying peace where there is no peace."
Some of them are sent by their tummies
I have neither known them nor sent them
and yet they say, "as surely as the Lord
  lives."
Behold the eye of God has seen your
  desolation
Countless prophets have I sent to this
  rebellious city
And yet you remain unrepentant

Woe to the city that slaughters Prophets,
mutilators of your own brother!
cursed is your land as been fed by the blood
   of the saints
You discriminate, as though you were
   permanent dwellers on earth
Don't you know that the earth is the Lord's
and He can wipe you out of sight and out of
   mind as He pleases
There are crowns in that land,
where the Prophets you murdered are
   crowned with gold and silver
Woe to my beloved city, for your gods
   cannot protect you
To captivity you shall go
And yet I have the righteous few, whom I
   have spared from calamity
Because they have not bowed to idols and
   they are under God's eye

I Am Unstoppable

Remember the days before I met him
Walking in the crowd, being influenced
  by the crowd
Filled with discord, discontentment
and discomforts,
complaints and comments on matters not
  understood
Commotions arose emotions,
as though contesting for promotion
I was young, naïve and stoppable
Many voices contested for my attention,
being pulled to wrong directions
tackling life in wrong dimensions
till I was lost within me and forgot my true
  identity
Being painted through my past errors and
  failures
Generational curses, poverty, idol worship,
I was defeated and stoppable.
Rejection paved my way to Salvation
I am a blessed nation
Being declared not guilty by my Father,
who may accuse me now and win
  thereafter?
Even the accuser of our brothers is not
  strong enough to defeat me
I am invincible.

The only power my accuser poses is to strike
  my heel,
to drive me closer to my Maker
Fully equipped on proper ways of handling
  God's weapons,
I have victory
The first level of conflict is Kingdom conflict
and the eternal Kingdom shall reign
The ancient serpent was hurled out of
  Heavens, by one Angel
For he is not God's equal
Don't give satan a footstool,
for his time on earth will soon vanish
a kingdom established on the Rock of Ages,
shall stand from eternity to eternity
I am a citizen of an unstoppable Kingdom
I am unstoppable.

Why Are You So Downcast Within Me, O My Soul?

Why are you so downcast within me o
my soul?
Look unto God and behold your light has
come
Why wonder about in dismay when he had
prepared your path ahead
why allow your foot to stray when the going
gets tough?
Blessed is he that looks to no men in times of
afflictions
He that cast not the yoke on men
for them that look unto the Lord shall
receive their strength
and mount high
in times of rejection and isolation they shall
recall,
"I have a friend who sticks closer than a
brother."
Why are you so downcast Within Me O my
soul?
Look unto God and draw your strength
Call unto thee in times of trouble and
tribulations
They that thirsts, come drink from the
streams of water and thirst no more

They that hunger, come buy freely, bread
  that satisfies
Why must you go on suffering when he
  stands waiting on your doorstep to soothe
  your pain?
Why are you so downcast Within Me O My
  Soul
Look unto God and find peace
Behold I stand in the door knocking, him
  that responds
I shall come in and dine with him
Why must you dine on the table of Belial,
  when your table is set in Heavenly
  realms?
Why must you be drunk with tears, when
  there is enough to drink without a single
  penny?
Why drink from the Cup of Sorrow, when
  there is freedom indeed?
Why are you so downcast within me O my
  soul?
Look unto God and live!

Walking in the Light

Countless days have I been walking in
   darkness?
All was good and all permitted, but none
   was helpful
Tribal marks on my forehead have stolen
   my virtue
Instead of granting wisdom,
This dark life filled with drugs, witchcraft,
   cults
and prostitution was too much with me.
So I choose to walk in the Light
Foundational curses and the witchcraft
   stronghold crippled my steps
and pulled me back to nothing,
when I knew I could be something.
Come to me they that are weary and heavy-
   laden,
rest content in the Light and walk in the
   Light
For Light is better than darkness,
Just as wisdom better than folly.
Light walked before them and lived among
   them
though, they could touch Him and feel him,
they understood Him not.
Some are ever hearing but never
   understanding
while others have seen, but never perceived.

Walk in the Light and walk in the Truth.
Are you free indeed or you still in need?
Find Peace and Live.
The dead shall rise and meet Him,
As light dawns in hades, to snatch those
  who slept in faith
Believing in the promised Son.
Walk in the Light and Live!

A Letter to my Husband

For I have believed,
  Before I have seen
I have hope, I can touch
Rest assured, I will touch
Caged by the rules and
regulations of present days' time,
Keeping us apart.
Take me to the palace,
Leave me there alone, by His doorstep
See if He opens up,
Let my spirit touch, the chords of your heart
Then my heart sings joy.
Miles and miles apart, yet in you I live
And you in me,
a mystery none may explain
in utter silence, thousands of smiles may be
  seen
This no man understands,
A reason why I write this letter to my
  husband.

41